HAIKUS
OF
ALL SEASONS VI

HUMANITY

MAYUMI ITOH

For the victims of the Minamata Disease

and

Ishimure Michiko (1927–2018)

who fought for the fishermen in Minamata

Contents

Note for paperback edition: This book is for on-demand

printing. The actual page numbers (and page breaks and

other formatting matters) may differ from the page numbers

shown in the Table of Contents above, due to the

formatting by Amazon that is used on the day of the book

order.

List of photographs

All photographs were taken by the author except for those whose sources are credited below. , taken by the author

Photograph 1. Footsteps in the snow, taken by the author

Photograph 2. Japanese weeping cherry tree branches covered with snow, taken by the author

Photograph 3. Emperor and empress hina dolls for Hina Doll Festival, taken by the author

Photograph 4. Statue of jizō bosatsu, the guardian god of unborn children and the mothers, taken by the author

Photograph 5. Carp streamers, under Creative Commons license, "Carp streamers, Fukusaki-chō, Hyōgo prefecture," May 5, 2006, https://commons.wikimedia.org/wiki/File:Koinobori01_2048.jpg

Photograph 6. Bearded iris, taken by the author

Photograph 7. Seashells, taken by the author

Notes on the Text

This book presents each haiku in both Japanese and English so that non-Japanese-speaking readers can fully appreciate it. The first page for a given haiku (on the left side) shows the original haiku in Japanese, which is made up of a combination of Chinese characters (*kanji*) and Japanese phonetic characters (*hiragana* and *katakana*). In accordance with the customs for writing haiku, the old spellings of *hiragana* are used for the original haiku.

Then, in order to facilitate a better understanding, especially for those who are studying Japanese, the original haiku is shown in a modern spelling in *hiragana* and *katakana*. This allows readers to see how the haiku is exactly pronounced phonetically. There are many ways to pronounce specific *kanji* words, and the original Japanese haiku does not indicate how each *kanji* word is actually pronounced. It is sometimes difficult even for Japanese readers to know the pronunciation. Therefore, the simpler

rendition of each haiku only in modern *hiragana* and

katakana will help.

Afterward, the identification of the season word for

the haiku is given and some explanations of the cultural and

historical backgrounds are added where applicable.

On the second page for a given haiku (on the right

side), a romanization of the original Japanese haiku is

provided, first, so that English-speaking readers can

understand how the haiku is pronounced. The words in

Roman letters are divided into smaller groups of syllables,

for easier reading.

Then, an English translation of the haiku is

presented. It is a paraphrasing of the haiku, rather than a

literal translation, in order for it to make the best sense in

English. Accordingly, for many cases, the word order of

the haiku might be different from the original haiku in

Japanese. It is followed by the English translations of the

season word and the explanations of the cultural and

historical backgrounds. This completes the presentation of

a given haiku.

All translations, including those of haikus, were

made by the author. For romanizing Japanese words, the

Hepburn style is primarily used, with macrons. However,

macrons are not used for words known in English without

macrons, as for Kyoto and Tokyo. Another exception is

that "n" is not converted to "m" for words where it

precedes "b, m, and p." Examples include tonbo, instead of

tombo; Gunma prefecture, instead of Gumma prefecture;

and tanpopo, instead of tampopo.

Names of Japanese persons are given with the

surname first, except for those who use the reversed order

in English. Honorific prefixes, such as doctor and mister,

are not used in the text, except in direct quotations.

Acknowledgments

I would like to thank all the members of *Hoshi no shima kukai* (the Haiku Society of Star Island, a new name for the Haiku Society of New York), past and present—including but not limited to Esaka Kinuyo, Hara Yasuko, Sakuhara Aya, and Tsukino Popona—as well as Tsuneo Akaha, Kent Calder, Toshiko Calder, Steve Clemons, Akiko Collcutt, Gerald Curtis, Joshua Fogel, Hoshi Hiroshi, Ronald Hrebenar, Ken Kawata, Donald Keene, Ellis Krauss, Mike Mochizuki, T. J. Pempel, Stephen Roddy, Gilbert Rozman, Richard Samuels, Vicki Wong, Donald Zagoria, and Quansheng Zhao, for continuous encouragement and inspirations. I extend my deep appreciation to Gregory Rewoldt and Meg Itoh for generous support.

Preface

This is the sixth haiku anthology by this author and embraces two of the seven major themes of haiku: 1) daily life or humanity; 2) events or observances, such as traditional seasonal events and religious ceremonies and rituals. As background information, this book introduces anecdotes about the culture and history of each subject, where applicable. For rules about haiku making, please see *Haikus of All Seasons I: The Heavens and The Earth* (2018).

This book is dedicated to the victims of the Minamata Disease, mercury poisoning by industrial waste dumped in the Shiranui (Yatsushiro) Sea, Kumamoto prefecture, as well as to Ishimure Michiko (1927–2018). The haikus for February feature them. Ishimure was a 'Japanese Rachel Carson.' She fought for the fishermen in Minamata, who had fallen victim to the Minamata Disease.

This was the first "public disease" caused by environmental pollution of the food chain.

The Japanese chemical company called Japan Chisso (current Chisso Corporation, "chisso" means nitrogen in Japanese) dumped its industrial waste in the Shiranui Sea, which otherwise had been blessed by its pristine natural beauty and abundant marine products. The symptoms of the mercury poisoning first appeared in cats in the locale, as they had eaten fish from the Shiranui Sea contaminated by methylmercury. In the early 1950's, cats began acting strangely as if mad (people referred to it as the "mad cat dance"), walked sideways, and died. The cats were like 'canaries in a coal mine.'

Nevertheless, there was no clear awareness or official recognition of the disease by the Japanese government, and human deaths followed. Cats and fishermen had coexisted in the fishing community—the former caught the mice that damaged fishing tools—and both fell victim to the disease.   The surviving fishermen had lost the only way of living they had known for generations.

In May 1956, Minamata City officially recognized the disease, but the Japan Chisso did not acknowledge its responsibilities. Thus, a series of arduous and dragged-out lawsuits against the company and the Japanese government ensued. A local poet, Ishimure Michiko, was deeply distressed with the environmental destruction of Shiranui Sea and its surrounding areas. She felt the pains and sorrows of the local people (and animals), as her own.

Ishimure thus courageously led the class-action lawsuits and supported the fishermen, demonstrating and sitting in front of the national diet in Tokyo. Ishimura also tried to raise public awareness of the Minamata Disease through writing. For this cause, she became a prolific writer and published many compelling and poignant stories about nature and the people of Shiranui.

On May 1, 2018, the 62-year anniversary day of the
official recognition of the Minamata Disease by Minamata
City, a memorial service for the victims of the disease was
held in front of their memorial stone in Minamata. There,
the Japan Chisso president stated, "I personally think that
the relief measures for the victims are already done and
complete." In response, the representative of the Shiranui
Society of Minamata Disease Patients stated, "This is a
desecration for the surviving victims. The company
executives are ignoring the reality in which the patients are
continuing their lawsuits, seeking relief." Thus, the
lawsuits go on.

Ishimure died on February 10, 2018. Her major
works include *Kugai jōdo: Waga Minamata-byō* (*lit.*, "The
Sea of Suffering and the Pure Land of Paradise: My
Minamata Disease"), *Ten no io* (*uo*) (*lit.*, "Fish in Heaven"),
and *Tsubaki no umi no ki* (*lit.*, "The Story of the Sea of
Camellias").

Sources

"Ishimure Michiko-san shikyo" (Ms. Ishimure Michiko dies), *Asahi Shimbun*, February 10, 2018.

"Minamata-byō 'kyūsai owatteiru' Chisso shachō hatsugen" (Chisso president says, "The Relief Measures for the Minamata Disease Are Done and Complete," *Tokyo Shimbun*, May 1, 2018.

Smith, W. Eugene, *Tomoko Uehara in Her Bath*, (photo essay), *Life Magazine*, June 2, 1972.

Ui, June, *Kōgai no seijigaku: Minamata-byō o otte* (Politics of Public Diseases: Chasing the Minamata Disease), Tokyo: Sanseidō, 1968.

January

Photograph 1. Footsteps in the snow, taken by the author

去年今年

　　残されし者

　　　　逝きし者

こぞことし

　　のこされしもの

　　　　ゆきしもの

季語　去年今年（こぞことし、新年）

Kozo kotoshi

nokosare shi mono

yuki shi mono

Last year and this year

those who have passed away

and those who are left behind

Season word: *kozo kotoshi* (*lit.*, "last year and the new

year," means thinking about the last year on New Year's

Day; signifies the new year)

初日記

　　パソコン開き

　　　　夜の白む

はつにっき

　　パソコンひらき

　　　　よのしらむ

季語　　初日記（新年）

Hatsu nikki

paso kon hiraki

yo no shiramu

The first diary entry of the new year

one opens a personal computer

and the night turns to dawn

Season word: *hatsu nikki* (first diary entry of the new year;

new year)

夢売りや

　　みすゞの初夢

　　　　叶へんと

ゆめうりや

　　みすゞのはつゆめ

　　　　かなえんと

季語　　初夢（新年）

女流詩人金子みすゞ（1903年−1930年）は、「夢売り」と
題する詩の中で、貧しい家の子供達に良い初夢を届けて
くれと「夢売り」に願う。

Yume uri ya

 Misuzu no hatsu yume

  kanaen to

The dream seller

 vowed to make Misuzu's dream on New Year's Day

  come true

Season word: *hatsu yume* (dream on New Year's Day; new
year)
The Japanese female poet Kaneko Misuzu (1903–1930)
wrote a poem, "Dream Seller," in which she wished that he
would visit the children of poor families so that they could
have fine dreams on New Year's Day.

初稽古

　　お琴の調べ

　　　　雪の聴く

はつげいご

　　おことのしらべ

　　　　ゆきのきく

季語　初稽古（新年）

この句は、厳密に言えば季重なりであるが、初稽古が主季

語で、雪（冬の季語）と齟齬がないので、許容される。

Hatsu geiko

o koto no shirabe

yuki no kiku

First practice of the new year

the snow listens

to the tune of the koto

Season word: *hatsu geiko* (first practice of the new year;

new year)

初競りや

　　築地最後の

　　　　大鮪

はつせりや

　　つきじさいごの

　　　　おおまぐろ

季語　　初競り（新年）

1935年に開設した築地魚市場は、長年の大論争の末、2018年10月6日に閉鎖されることに決定した。従って、2018年1月15日の初競りが、同市場最後の初競りとなり、関係者に深い感慨をもたらした。

Hatsu seri ya

    Tsukiji saigo no

        ō maguro

At the first bidding of the new year

    at the Tsukiji Fish Market

        a bidder obtained the last huge tuna fish

Season word: *hatsu seri* (first bidding of the new year; new year)

The Tsukiji Fish Market in Tokyo that had opened in 1935 closed in October 2018. The first bidding of this year at the market on January 5, 2018 marked the last *hatsu seri* there, filled with memories of this venerable institution.

初雪や

　　散歩の足を

　　　　黒く染め

はつゆきや

　　さんぽのあしを

　　　　くろくそめ

季語　初雪（冬）

Hatsu yuki ya

sanpo no ashi o

kuroku some

The first snow

is dyeing the footsteps

black

Season word: *hatsu yuki* (first snow of the season, winter)

雪祭り

　　松明に舞ふ

　　　　緋能面

ゆきまつり

　　たいまつにまう

　　　　ひのうめん

季語　雪祭り(冬)

長野県阿南町新野で、毎年1月14日－15日に行う五穀豊

穣を祈る雪祭り。伊豆神社で夜通し続く神の舞は、田楽や

猿楽の起源と言われる。緋色の能面は、五穀豊穣を司る

幸法(さいほう)という神の舞に着用する。

Yuki matsuri

taimatsu ni mau

hi nōmen

During the snow festival

the red Noh mask is dancing

among the flaming torches

Season word: *yuki matsuri* (snow festival; winter)

The highlight of the snow festival in Niino, Anan-chō,

Nagano prefecture, held annually on January 14–15, is the

all-night dances of god figures, including one wearing a red

Noh mask, praying for a good harvest for the year.

細雪

　　「朝光」となり

　　　　母の逝く

ささめゆき

　　ちょうこうとなり

　　　　ははのゆく

季語　細雪（冬）

「朝光」は、母の戒名の一部。

Sasame yuki

    Chōkō to nari

        haha no yuku

In fine, light snow

    my mother passed away

        and became the Morning Light

Season word: *sasame yuki* (fine, light snow; winter)

My mother passed away on January 12, 2010. Part of her

Buddhist afterlife (posthumous) name is Chōko, which

means, "morning light."

雪の夜は

　　忘れ形見の

　　　　寝巻着て

ゆきのよは

　　わすれがたみの

　　　　ねまききて

季語　雪(冬)

Yuki no yo wa

    wasure gatami no

        nemaki kite

In the night of snow

    one wears the night robe

        that the dead mother used to wear

Season word: *yuki* (snow; winter)

「寒晒し

　　蕎麦」を育む

　　　水の音

かんざらし

　　そばをはぐくむ

　　　みずのおと

季語　寒晒し（冬）

長野県の蕎麦生産者は、蕎麦をより美味しくするため1月に10日間、蕎麦の実を清流に晒す。これを「寒晒し蕎麦」と呼ぶ。

Kan zarashi

    soba o hagukumu

        mizu no oto

The buckwheat

    is being tended

        by the sound of the cold river

Season word: *kan-zarashi soba* (buckwheat having been

soaked in the cold river; winter)

In Nagao prefecture, buckwheat noodle producers go out of

their way to soak the buckwheat in the cold river for ten

days in January so that the buckwheat noodles have a

strong and sweet flavor.

February

Photograph 2. Japanese weeping cherry tree branches

covered with snow, taken by the author

春の風

　　猫に誘はれ

　　　　水俣へ

はるのかぜ

　　ねこにさそMPHわれ

　　　　みなまたへ

季語　　春の風（春）

熊本県天草下島（しもしま）生まれの石牟礼道子（1927年
−2018年）は、水俣で猫に接することによって後に「水俣
病」と命名される異変に気づく。2月の俳句は、水俣病の
犠牲者および2月10日に亡くなった石牟礼道子を追悼。

Haru no kaze

    neko ni sasoware

        Minamata e

The spring wind

    the cat invites

        one to Minamata

Season word: *haru no kaze* (spring wind; spring)

Ishimure Michiko (1927–2018) was born in Shimoshima, the largest island of the Amakusa (*lit.*, "heaven grass") Islands, which are separated by the Yatsushiro Sea from the rest of Kumamoto prefecture, including Minamata. She observed the strange behavior of cats in Minamata and noticed the mercury poisoning, which became known as the Minamata Disease.

水俣の

　　猫狂ひ

　　　　春海荒れ狂ふ

みなまたの

　　ねこくるい

　　　　しゅんかいあれくるう

季語　春海（春）

熊本県の水俣病は、水銀に汚染された魚を食べた猫が横

歩きなどの異常行動をきたして（「猫の狂い踊り」）狂死した

ことから認識されるようになった。2月22日は、「猫の日」。

Minamata no

    neko kurui

        shunkai are kuruu

The cat in Minamata

    went mad

        and the spring sea was enraged

Season word: *shunkai* (spring sea; spring)

In the early 1950's, cats in Minamata walked sideways, acted

strangely as if mad ('mad cat dance'), and died. They had eaten

fish from the Shiranui (Yatsushiro) Sea, the inner sea of

Minamata, contaminated by industrial waste. The cats were like

'canaries in a coal mine.' February 22 is the Day of Cats.

不知火の

　　漁師の呻き

　　　　春の空

しらぬいの

　　りょうしのうめき

　　　　はるのそら

季語　　春の空（春）

不知火（八代海）の漁師は猫と共存してきた。漁に猫を連れ、漁具を荒らす鼠を取らせて褒美に魚を与えた。猫と共に、漁師も水銀中毒の犠牲となった。不知火は「有明海と八代海の沖に陰暦8月1日前後の夜中に無数の火が明滅し揺らめく現象」としては秋の季語であるが、この場合は季語として使われていない。

Shiranui no

   ryōshi no umeki

      haru no sora

In Shiranui

   the fishermen groan

      to the spring sky

Season word: *haru no sora* (spring sky; spring)

Cats and fishermen had coexisted in Shiranui, as the former caught the mice that damaged fishing tools. After cats had died with the mercury poisoning, the deaths of fishermen followed. Thus, both fell victim to the Minamata Disease.

海のみぞ知る

　　漁民の傷み

　　　　春の海

うみのみぞしる

　　ぎょみんのいたみ

　　　　はるのうみ

季語　　春の海(春)

水俣病が水俣市によって公式に認められたのは、1956年のことであった。その後、水俣病は食物連鎖の環境汚染による初の「公害」と認定された。

Umi nomi zo shiru

　　gyomin no itami

　　　　haru no umi

Only the sea knows

　　the pains of the fishermen

　　　　in the spring sea

Season word: *haru no umi* (spring sea; spring)

The Minamata Disease was officially recognized by

Minamata City in 1956. This is the first "public disease"

caused by environmental pollution of the food chain.

春雷や

　　不知火の歎き

　　　　轟きて

しゅんらいや

　　しらぬいのなげき

　　　　とどろきて

季語　春雷（春）

Shunrai ya

Shiranui no nageki

todoroki te

The spring thunder and lightning

the lament of Shiranui

roars

Season word: *shunrai* (spring thunder and lightning;

spring)

春浅き

　　水俣の

　　　　ジャンヌ・ダルク逝く

はるあさき

　　みなまたの

　　　　ジャンヌ・ダルクゆく

季語　　春浅き（春）

2018年2月10日に亡くなった詩人・作家、石牟礼道子は、

『沈黙の春』のレイチェル・カーソン（1907年−1964年）と同様、

著作を通じて環境汚染・環境破壊に警鐘を鳴らした。さらに石

牟礼は、「公害」に敢然と立ち向かい、漁民とともに闘った。

Haru asaki

    Minamata no

        Jan'nu daruku yuku

In early spring

    the Jeanne d'Arc of Minamata

        passed away

Season word: *haru asaki* (early spring; spring)

The poet/writer Ishimure Michiko (1927–2018) died on February 10. She was a 'Japanese Rachel Carson' and selflessly fought for the fishermen in Minamata, who had fallen victim to the Minamata Disease.

不知火の

　　涙や春の

　　　　海となり

しらぬいの

　　なみだやはるの

　　　　うみとなり

季語　　春の海（春）

不知火は八代海の別名で、水俣の内海である。

Shiranui no

    namida ya haru no

        umi to nari

The tears

    of Shiranui

        have become the spring sea

Season word: *haru no umi* (spring sea; spring)

All the communities in Shiranui (Yatsushiro) Sea are
mourning the death of Ishimure Michiko.

春の風

　　『苦海浄土』の

　　　　書を捲る

はるのかぜ

　　くがいじょうどの

　　　　しょをめくる

季語　春の風（春）

漁師と生き、共に闘った石牟礼道子の代表作に『苦海浄
土　わが水俣』等がある。

Haru no kaze

    Kugai jōdo no

        sho o mekuru

The spring wind

    is turning the pages

        of Kugai jōdo

Season word: *haru no kaze* (spring wind; spring)

One of the definitive works of Ishimure Michiko is *Kugai jōdo: Waga Minamata-byō* (*lit.*, "The Sea of Suffering and the Pure Land of Paradise: My Minamata Disease").

水俣の

　　語り部逝きて

　　　　椿泣く

みなまたの

　　かたりべゆきて

　　　　つばきなく

季語　椿（春）

石牟礼道子の著書、『椿の海の記』に寄せて。

Minamata no

    kataribe yukite

        tsubaki naku

The storyteller of Minamata

    is gone

        and the camellia is sobbing

Season word: *tsubaki* (camellia; spring)

Ishimure Michiko wrote many compelling stories about nature and the people of Shiranui. They include *Tsubaki no umi no ki* (*lit.*, "The Story of the Sea of Camellias").

不知火の

　　花藻の涙

　　　　流れゆく

しらぬいの

　　はなものなみだ

　　　　ながれゆく

季語　　海の花藻（春）

「花藻」（藻の花）は、本来、淡水藻の花の総称で、夏の季
語であるが、海の藻の花は春に咲くので、春の季語となる。
この句は、不知火の海の花藻を詠んだもの。

Shiranui no

hanamo no namida

nakare yuku

The seaweed flowers

in Shiranui

their tears are floating on the sea

Season word: *umi no hanamo* (seaweed flowers; spring)

Ishimure Michiko wrote about seaweed flowers in her

poems. The "*hanamo*" (aquaplant flower) is a season word

of summer. By contrast, seaweed flower blooms in spring

and signifies spring. This haiku refers to seaweed flowers

because they grow in the Shiranui Sea.

March

Photograph 3. Emperor and empress hina dolls for Hina

Doll Festival, taken by the author

鄙びたる

　　内裏に宿る

　　　　祖母の霊

ひなびたる

　　だいりにやどる

　　　　そぼのれい

季語　内裏（内裏雛、春）

桃の節句に祖母が孫娘に雛人形セットを与える伝統。

Hina bitaru

    dairi ni yadoru

        sobo no rei

The old emperor and empress hina dolls

    embrace

        the soul of the dead grandmother

Season word: *dairi* (*dairi bina*, emperor and empress *hina*

dolls; spring)

It is a custom for a grandmother to give her granddaughter a set of *hina*

dolls of the emperor the empress and their attendants (older sets even

had a miniature model of the imperial court), displayed at home during

the Hina Doll Festival season (Girls' Day is March 3), in order to pray

for the healthy growth and happiness of her granddaughter.

吊るし雛

　　　願ふ数ほど

　　　　　長くなり

つるしびな

　　　ねがうかずほど

　　　　　ながくなり

季語　　吊るし雛（春）

吊るし雛は、雛壇飾りに代わって作られた、特定の地方の
伝統。

Tsurushi bina

negau kazu hodo

nagaku nari

The hanging hina doll

is getting longer

as the number of wishes for the granddaughter increases

Season word: *tsurushi bina* (hanging *hina* dolls; spring)

In some locales, grandmothers could not afford an expensive *hina* doll set, and instead made handmade *hina* dolls and other art objects, tie them in a string, and hang them indoors or outdoors for the Hina Doll Festival.

白酒や

　　三人官女の

　　　　深夜会

しろざけや

　　さんにんかんじょの

　　　　しんやかい

季語　白酒（春）　三人官女（三人官女雛、春）

Shiro zake ya

   san'nin kanjo no

      shin'ya kai

Sweet white sake

   the three ladies-in-waiting dolls

      are having a midnight party

Season words: *shiro zake* (sweet white sake; spring) and

san'nin kanjo (three ladies-in-waiting *hina* dolls; spring)

It is a tradition to have a sip of sweet white sake to

celebrate the Hina Doll Festival.

お水取り

　　松明駆け抜け

　　　響く鐘

おみずとり

　　たいまつかけぬけ

　　　ひびくかね

季語　　お水取り（春）

3月1日−14日（旧暦2月1−15日）に東大寺二月堂の修

二会では薬玉のような巨大な松明が二月堂の回廊を駆け

抜け、最後には回廊から打ち振られ火の粉となって散る。

O mizu tori

    taimatsu kake nuke

        hibiku kane

During the Water Ceremony

    the flaming torches dash along the temple balcony

        and the sound of the giant bell reverberates

Season word: *O-mizu tori* (the Water Ceremony at Tōdai

Temple; spring)

Burning giant torches (the Fire Ceremony) is part of the Water

Ceremony at Tōdai Temple. It is the Buddhist ritual of driving

away evil spirits and praying for a good harvest for the year.

The ceremony was conducted at Nigatsu-dō (February Hall), on

February 1–15 in the lunar calendar, and now on March 1–14.

阿智の村

　　湯屋守様の

　　　　お焚き上げ

あちのむら

　　ゆやもりさまの

　　　　おたきあげ

季語　　湯屋守様のお焚き上げ（春）

長野県阿智村では、12月から2月まで神様が昼神温泉郷で冬
籠りするという信仰があり、その神様を湯屋守様と呼ぶ。3月3日
の夜、15体の藁製の湯屋守様（人の形をした松明）を炊き上げ
て、冬の間見守ってくれた湯屋守様を天に返す行事を行う。

Achi no mura

    Yuya mori sama no

        o taki age

Achi village

    is conducting

        the burning ritual for the Yuyamori gods

Season word: *Yuyamori-sama no o-takiage* (burning ritual

for the Yuyamori gods; spring)

On the night of March 3, the folk in Achi village, Nagano

prefecture, conducts a ritual of burning fire in order to send

off the Shinto gods who had wintered in the hot spring.

梅の香や

　　祈願の札を

　　　　結びたり

うめのかや

　　きがんのふだを

　　　　むすびたり

季語　梅(春)

Ume no ka ya

    kigan no fuda o

        musubi tari

In the scent of plum blossoms

    a student has tied

        a prayer tag

Season word: *ume* (plum blossoms; spring)

It is a custom for students to visit shrines and write their

wish on a wooden plaque or a paper tag in order to pray for

passing the entrance exams of the schools to which they

had applied.

光笑む

　　病室の窓

　　　　春を知る

ひかりえむ

　　びょうしつのまど

　　　　はるをしる

季語　春(春)

Hikari emu

 byōshitsu no mado

  haru o shiru

The gentle light

 lets the hospital window

  know of the arrival of spring

Season word: *haru* (spring; spring)

This scene metaphorically describes the patients in the
hospital watching the window.

黄水仙

　　左手使ふ

　　　　父を看る

きずいせん

　　ひだりてつかう

　　　　ちちをみる

季語　黄水仙（春）

脳梗塞で倒れ、リハビリ中の父。

Ki zuisen

hidari te tsukau

chichi o miru

The yellow daffodil

looks after the father

who is using his left hand

Season word: *ki zuisen* (yellow daffodils; spring)

The right hand of the father was paralyzed by a stroke.

卒業式

　　見送る母の

　　　　影細し

そつぎょうしき

　　みおくるははの

　　　　かげほそし

季語　卒業式（春）

Sotsugyō shiki

miokuru haha no

kage hosho shi

At the graduation ceremony

the shadow of the mother

looks thin

Season word: *sotsugyō shiki* (school graduation ceremony; spring)

The Japanese school year ends in March.

利休忌や

　　黒樂茶碗

　　　　なほ黒し

りきゅうきや

　　くろらくちゃわん

　　　　なおくろし

季語　利休忌（春）

千利休（1522年−1591年）は、旧暦2月28日に自害した
とされる（自害せずに生きていたという新説あり）。黒樂は
利休好み。今日、利休ゆかりの京都・大徳寺と表千家茶
道では新暦3月27日に利休忌を行う。

Rikyū ki ya

kuro raku chawan

nao kuro shi

On the memorial day of Sen no Rikyū

the black Raku tea bowl

looks even more black

Season word: *Rikyū-ki* (anniversary memorial day of Sen

no Rikyū's death, March 27; spring).

This is a homage to the master of the tea ceremony, Sen no Rikyū

(1522–1591), who committed suicide on February 28 in the lunar

calendar. He perfected a minimalist style and favored black Raku

tea bowls. Today, Daitoku Temple in Kyoto and the Omote Sen-ke

Tea Ceremony School conduct his memorial service on March 27.

April

Photograph 4. Statue of jizō bosatsu, the guardian god of

unborn children and their mothers, taken by the author

お遍路や

　　野辺の地蔵の

　　　　見守りて

おへんろや

　　のべのじぞうの

　　　　みまもりて

季語　　お遍路（春）

O henro ya

    nobe no jizō no

        mimamori te

The spring pilgrim

    is being watched over

        by jizō in the field

Season word: *o-henro* (spring pilgrim to temples; spring)

The most famous spring pilgrim route is the Shikoku Henro of visiting the 88 Temples on Shikoku Island. Jizō (jizō bosatsu) refers to the stone statues of the guardian gods of unborn children and their mothers.

春姫の

　　お輿入れ

　　　　花の迎へる

はるひめの

　　おこしいれ

　　　　はなのむかえる

季語　　花（桜、詩歌の世界では花は桜を指す、春）

尾張藩初代藩主徳川義直（徳川家康の九男）に13歳（数え年）で嫁

いだ紀州藩初代藩主浅野幸長（よしなが）の娘、春姫（1603年−163

7年）の名古屋城本丸御殿への輿入れの行列は、壮大・華麗であった。

これは、戦国時代が終わり、太平の世が到来したことの象徴でもあっ

た。この「春姫道中」が、名古屋の豪華な結婚式の起源と言われる。

Haru hime no

    o koshi ire

        hana no mukaeru

Princess Haru

    her wedding procession

        is being welcomed by cherry blossoms

Season word: *hana* (*lit.*, "flower" refers to cherry blossoms

in haiku; spring)

In 1615, Haruhime (1603–1637), the daughter of the first lord of

the Kii province, Asano Yoshinaga, was wed to the first lord of

the Owari province, Tokugawa Yoshinao, the ninth son of Ieyasu.

Her wedding procession on foot to the Nagoya Castle Main

Palace was grand, marking the arrival of peaceful times.

清明節

　　中山陵の

　　　　参拝者

せいめいせつ

　　ちゅうざんりょうの

　　　　さんぱいしゃ

季語　清明節（春）

清明節は、中国の墓の大掃除日。日本の春の彼岸参りに

相当する。中山陵は、南京にある孫文（1866年－1925年）

の廟。2018年の清明節は、4月5日である。

Seimei setsu

Chūzan ryō no

Sanpai sha

On the Tomb Sweeping Day

there is a visitor

at the Mausoleum of Sun Yat-sen

Season word: *Seimei-setsu* (Tomb Sweeping Day,

Qingming Festival; spring)

The Tomb Sweeping Day in China falls on the 15th day after the

spring equinox. It is April 5 for 2018. This is equivalent to the

Japanese custom of visiting ancestral tombs on the vernal and

autumnal equinoxes. The Mausoleum of Sun Yat-sen (1866–

1925) is located in Nanjing, China.

「邯鄲の夢」

　　破れ果て

　　　　桜散る

かんたんのゆめ

　　やぶれはて

　　　　さくらちる

季語　桜散る（春）

唐の歴史家・小説家、沈既済（750年−800年頃）作の『枕中記』にある故事の一つ。別名、「盧生の夢」。

Kantan no yume

    yabure hate

        sakura chiru

The Dream of Kantan

    was broken

        and the cherry blossoms are falling

Season word: *sakura chiru* (cherry blossoms fall; spring)

The Dream of Kantan (Handan in Chinese) refers to a story in the Pillow Story by Shen Jiji (750–circa 800), in which a Daoist monk in Handan lends a young man a pillow and through a dream makes him realize the ephemerality of life and the futility of pursuing fortune and fame.

花吹雪

　　娘の門出

　　　花開く

はなふぶき

　　むすめのかどで

　　　はなひらく

季語　花吹雪（春）

Hana fubuki

musume no kadode

hana hiraku

In the cherry blossom shower

the new life of the daughter

has just begun

Season word: *hana fubuki* (*lit.*, "cherry blossom shower,"

falling cherry blossoms; spring)

母子草

　　亡き母の歳

　　　　数へたり

ははこぐさ

　　なきははのとし

　　　　かぞえたり

季語　母子草（春）

Hahako gusa

    naki haha no toshi

        kazoe tari

The Jersey cudweed

    is counting

        the would-be age of the dead mother

Season word: *hahako gusa* (Jersey cudweed; spring)

Hahako gusa literally means "mother-child grass."

春の風

　　自転車に乗る

　　　植物図鑑

はるのかぜ

　　じてんしゃにのる

　　　しょくぶつずかん

季語　春の風（春）

Haru no kaze

    jitensha ni noru

        shokubutsu zukan

In the spring wind

    the illustrated plant book

        is riding on the bicycle

Season word: *haru no kaze* (spring wind; spring)

It is fun to ride a bicycle to a field in the spring with an illustrated plant book and find out the names of each plant there.

蓬摘む

　　人は等しく

　　　　和人なり

よもぎつむ

　　ひとはひとしく

　　　　わじんなり

季語　　蓬摘む（春）

米国で雑草と見なされているヨモギを摘むのは、蓬餅を作
る日本人のみであろう。

Yomogi tsumu

    hito wa hitoshiku

        wajin nari

Those who are

    picking up mugwort

        are all Japanese

Season word: *yomogi* (mugwort; spring)

Japanese collect this pervasive wild grass on the hills that

nobody else would care to pick and make *yomogi mochi* (or

kusa mochi), the rice cake flavored with the mugwort

leaves.

香合を

　　並べる師と弟子　　　85

　　　　沈丁花

こうごうを

　　ならべるしとでし

　　　　じんちょうげ

季語　沈丁花（春）春

4月18日は、「お香の日」。

Kōgō o

    naraberu shi to deshi

        jinchōge

The master of the incense ceremony and his student

    are arranging incense cases

        and the fragrant daphne watches

Season word: *jinchōge* (*daphne odora*; spring)

April 18 is designated as the Day of Incense in Japan.

潮干狩

　　光に跳ねる

　　　　稚児の声

しおひがり

　　ひかりにはねる

　　　　ちごのこえ

季語　潮干狩（春）

古くは、潮干狩は陰暦3月3日の行事であった。

Shio higari

   hikari ni haneru

      chigo no koe

At the clam digging

   the voice of the children

      is bouncing in the sunlight

Season word: *shiohi gari* (clam digging; spring)

Clam digging used to be an event conducted on March 3 in the lunar calendar.

May

Photograph 5. Carp streamers, under Creative Commons

license, "Carp streamers, Fukusaki-chō, Hyōgo prefecture,"

May 5, 2006,

https://commons.wikimedia.org/wiki/File:Koinobori01_2048.jpg

石鹸玉

　　虹色の夢

　　　　弾けたり

しゃぼんだま

　　にじいろのゆめ

　　　　はじけたり

季語　　石鹸玉(春)

Shabon dama

    niji iro no yume

        hajike tari

Soap bubbles

    the dream in rainbow colors

        bursts

Season word: *shabon dama* (soap bubbles; spring)

母子家庭

　　菫の匂ふ

　　　　置き手紙

ぼしかてい

　　すみれのにおう

　　　　おきてがみ

季語　菫(春)

Boshi katei

　　sumire no niou

　　　　oki tegami

The single mother

　　leaves a note with the scent of violets

　　　　to her child

Season words: *sumire* (violets; spring)

遅き春

　　同窓会の

　　　　案内来る

おそきはる

　　どうそうかいの

　　　　あないくる

季語　　遅き春（春）

Osoki haru

dōsō kai no

anai kuru

In late spring

the invitation to a school alumni reunion

has arrived

Season word: *osoki haru* (late spring; spring)

勿忘草

　　心の詩織に

　　　　挟みたり

わすれなぐさ

　　こころのしおりに

　　　　はさみたり

季語　勿忘草(春)

Wasure na gusa

kokoro no shiori ni

hasami tari

One tucks

the forget-me-not into the heart

as a bookmark

Season word: *wasure na gusa* (forget-me-nots; spring)

鯉のぼり

　　金の鯱鉾

　　　見上げたり

こいのぼり

　　きんのしゃちほこ

　　　みあげたり

季語　　鯉幟（こいのぼり、夏）

「尾張名古屋は城で保（も）つ」と歌われた名古屋城は、金
の鯱鉾で有名。俳句では、5月5日から夏となる。従って、
端午の節句に飾る鯉幟は、夏の季語となる。

Koi nobori

    kin no shachi hoko

        miage tari

The carp streamer

    is looking up

        at the golden statues of orcas

Season word: *koi nobori* (carp streamer; summer)

Japanese hoist carp streamers for the Boys' Festival (May 5) praying for the healthy growth and happiness of the boys. For haiku, summer begins on May 5 and therefore carp streamers signify summer. A pair of golden statues of orcas adorn Nagoya Castle in Nagoya, Aichi prefecture, dominating the sky.

名古屋城

　　天守見納め

　　　　夏の空

なごやじょう

　　てんしゅみおさめ

　　　　なつのそら

季語　　夏の空（夏）

2018年5月、木造復元工事のため名古屋城の天守閣が閉鎖
された。名古屋城は、1930年に城郭として初めて国宝に指定
されたが、1945年5月太平洋戦争の空襲で本丸御殿・天守閣
とも焼失した。1959年10月に鉄筋コンクリートの天守閣が再建
されたが、老朽化のため、木造復元事業が発足した。戦後の復
興を見守ってきた天守閣に名残を惜しむ長蛇の列ができた。

Nagoya jō

    tenshu miosame

      natsu no sora

Nagoya Castle

    its tower was seen for the last time

      under the summer sky

Season word: *natsu no sora* (summer sky; summer)

In May 2018, the tower of Nagoya Castle was closed to the public. The castle was designated as a National Treasure in 1930 but was destroyed by the U.S. air raids in 1945. A reinforced-concrete tower was built in 1959, but it has become old and will not stand up to earthquakes. A project to build a wooden tower, as in the original form, began. People flocked to see the tower for the last time, which had watched over the postwar reconstruction of the city.

余花探ね

　　遥かに響く

　　　　杖の音

よかたずね

　　はるかにひびく

　　　　つえのおと

季語　余花（夏）

余花は、初夏に入ってまだ咲き残っている桜のこと。

Yoka tazune

haruka ni hibiku

tsue no oto

In search of the remaining cherry blossoms

the sound of a stick

reverberates far away

Season word: *yoka* (the remaining cherry blossoms;

summer)

母の日や

　　花屋の女主

　　　　花貰ひ

ははのひや

　　はなやのあるじ

　　　　はなもらい

季語　母の日（夏）

花屋の女店主も母親である。

Haha no hi ya

   hana ya no aruji

      hana morai

On Mother's Day

   the proprietress of the flower shop

      is given flowers

Season word: *Haha no hi* (Mother's Day; summer)

The proprietress of the flower shop is also a mother.

母の日に

　香水試し

　　合ふ母子

ははのひに

　こうすいためし

　　あうははこ

季語　母の日（夏）

Haha no hi ni

    kōsui tameshi

        au haha ko

On Mother's Day

    the mother and the daughter

        are trying a new perfume

Season word: *Haha no hi* (Mother's Day; summer)

すれ違ふ

　　親子の想ひ

　　　　母の日よ

すれちがう

　　おやこのおもい

　　　　ははのひよ

季語　　母の日（夏）

子供の成長とともに、親子の間の考えの違いも大きくなる

ことを母の日に実感する。

Sure chigau

   oyako no omoi

      haha no hi yo

On Mother's Day

   incompatible expectations

      between the parent and the child loom larger

Season word: *Haha no hi* (Mother's Day; summer)

June

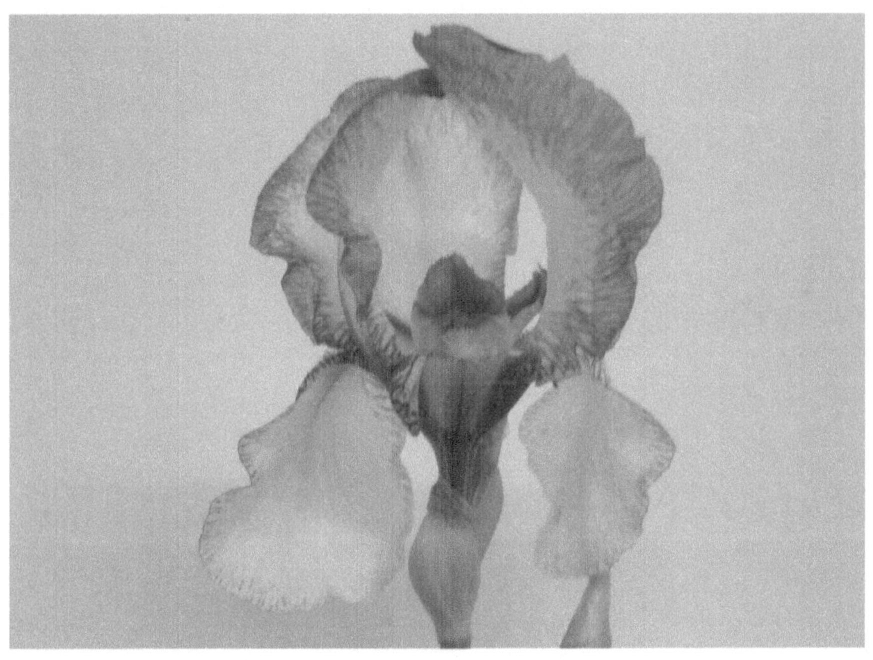

Photograph 6. Bearded iris, taken by the author

ゴッホ展

　　アヤメ畑の

　　　　夢見たり

ゴッホてん

　　アヤメばたけの

　　　　ゆめみたり

季語　アヤメ（夏）

フィンセント・ファン・ゴッホ（1853年−1890年）の油彩画

「アイリス」にちなんで。

Gohho ten

ayame batake no

yume mitari

After the van Gogh Exhibition

one is dreaming

of the field of irises

Season word: *ayame* (iris; summer)

This is a homage to the several oil paintings entitled, Irises,

by Vincent van Gogh (1853–1890).

彷徨ひ人

　　梅檀の香に

　　　　導かれ

さすらいびと

　　せんだんのかに

　　　　みちびかれ

季語　梅檀（センダン、夏）

Sasurai bito

    sendan no ka ni

        michibi kare

The traveler

    is being guided by the scent

        of the Chinaberry blossoms

Season word: *sendan* (Chinaberry blossoms; summer)

ローズ・ティー

　　二つの顔と

　　　　花びらと

ローズ・ティー

　　ふたつのかおと

　　　　はなびらと

季語　ローズ・ティー（夏）

Rōzu tii

futatsu no kao to

hana bira to

In the rose tea

two faces are floating in the teacup

along with the flower petals

Season word: *rōzu tii* (rose tea; summer)

若竹煮

　　青空覗く

　　　　五合庵

わかたけに

　　あおぞらのぞく

　　　　ごごうあん

季語　若竹煮（夏）

良寛和尚（1758年－1831年）の五合庵での竹の子の逸
話に寄せて。

Wakatake ni

aozora nozoku

Gogō an

Cooking bamboo shoots

the blue sky is peeking

at the Gogō Hut

Season word: *wakatake ni* (cooked bamboo shoots;

summer).

The Gogō Hut refers to a hermitage of the benevolent Zen

Buddhist monk Ryōkan (1758–1831). He is known for an

episode in which he made a hole in the floor of his hut so that the

bamboo shoot could keep growing. He then made a hole in the

roof so that the bamboo could grow further.

梅雨の朝

　　雨傘達の

　　　　ラッシュ・アワー

つゆのあさ

　　あまがさたちの

　　　　ラッシュ・アワー

季語　梅雨（夏）

Tsuyu no asa

amagasa tachi no

rasshu awā

The morning in the rainy season

the umbrellas

are caught in the rush hour

Season word: *tsuyu* (rainy season; summer)

紫陽花や

　　一色足りぬ

　　　　虹の橋

あじさいや

　　ひといろたりぬ

　　　　にじのはし

季語　　紫陽花（夏）　虹（夏）

石牟礼道子最期の連載「魂の秘境から」（朝日新聞）の中

「不知火の海の色が紫色の夕焼け空になったのは、一色

足りぬ虹の橋がかかったせいではなかろうか」に寄せて。

Ajisai ya

hito iro tarinu

niji no hashi

The hydrangea is watching

the rainbow bridge

that is missing one color

Season words: *ajisai* (hydrangea; summer) and *niji*

(rainbow; summer)

This is a homage to Ishimure Michiko's last series of

essays in the *Asahi Shimbun*, "From My Secret Soul," in

which she wrote "I wonder if the Sea of Shiranui turned a

purple sunset color because the rainbow missed one color."

黴ついた

　　アルバム見入る

　　　　雨の音

かびついた

　　アルバムみいる

　　　　あめのおと

季語　　黴（夏）

Kabi tsuita

   arubamu miiru

      ame no oto

The sound of the rain

   is penetrating

      the moldy old album

Season word: *kabi* (mold; summer)

桜桃忌

　　自己陶酔と

　　　　自暴自棄の死

おうとうき

　　じことうすいと

　　　　じぼうじきのし

季語　「桜桃忌」（6月19日、夏）

太宰治（1909年−1948年）は、6月13日に山崎富栄と入

水自殺したが、遺体が発見されたのは6月19日。この日は

奇しくも太宰の誕生日であったことから、晩年の短編小説

『桜桃』にちなんで、この日を「桜桃忌」と命名した。

Ōtō ki

    jiko tōsui to

       jibō jiki no shi

The cherry

    mourns the death

       of the self-indulgent and self-destructive writer

Season word: *Ōtō-ki* (*lit.*, "cherry memorial day," the memorial day of Dazai Osamu's death, June 19; summer) The novelist Dazai Osamu (1909–1948) committed double suicide with his lover on June 13, after writing a short story, *Ōtō* (*lit.*, "cherry"). Their bodies were discovered on June 19, which happened to be his birthday. Hence, June 19 was designated as his anniversary memorial day, which was named after the cherry.

「若葉中」

　　同窓の胸の

　　　　若葉かな

わかばちゅう

　　どうそうのむねの

　　　　わかばかな

季語　若葉（夏）

「若葉中」は実在する中学校。

Wakaba chū

doso no mune no

wakaba kana

The alumni of Wakaba Middle School

are wearing a badge

of young leaves on their collars

Season word: *wakaba* (young leaves; summer)

Wakaba Middle School actually exists.

草笛や

　　風の色聴く

　　　　蒼き空

くさぶえや

　　かぜのいろきく

　　　　あおきそら

季語　草笛（夏）

Kusa bue ya

kaze no iro kiku

aoki sora

The reed pipe

is listening to the color of the wind

in the pale blue sky

Season word: *kusa bue* (reed pipe; summer)

July

Photograph 7. Seashells, taken by the author

夏の海

　　貝殻拾ふ

　　　　風を撫で

なつのうみ

　　かいがらひろう

　　　　かぜをなで

季語　夏の海（夏）

Natsu no umi

    kaigawa hirou

        kaze o nade

The summer sea

    is gently touching the wind

        that is collecting seashells

Season word: *natsu no umi* (summer sea; summer)

海開き

　　ビキニ姿の

　　　　甲羅干し

うみびらき

　　ビキニすがたの

　　　　こうらぼし

季語　海開き（夏）

Umi biraki

bikini sugata no

kōra boshi

The beach opening

bikinis are sunbathing

looking like tortoise shells

Season word: *umi biraki* (beach opening; summer)

母遺し

　　梅干し届き

　　　　空青し

ははのこし

　　うめぼしとどき

　　　　そらあおし

季語　梅干し（夏）

Haha nokoshi

    umeboshi todoki

        sora aoshi

The pickled plums

    the dead mother made long years ago

        arrived from the blue sky

Season word: *ume boshi* (pickled plums; summer)

My sister found the pickled plums that my mother had

made years ago and sent them to the United States.

冷麦を

　　茹でる背中や

　　　　空の母

ひやむぎを

　　ゆでるせなかや

　　　　そらのはは

季語　　冷麦（夏）

Hiya mugi o

yuderu senaka ya

sora no haha

The cold noodles

the back of the mother making them long ago

appeared in the sky

Season word: *hiya mugi* (cold noodles; summer)

インデペンデンス・デイ

歴史刻みし

　　星条旗

インデペンデンス・デイ

れきしきざみし

　　せいじょうき

季語　インデペンデンス・デイ（7月4日、夏）

Independensu dei

rekishi kizami shi

seijōki

On Independence Day

the Stars and Stripes are flying

engraving history

Season word: *Independensu dei* (Independence Day, July

Fourth; summer)

ハンモック

　　異国の風を

　　　　揺らしたり

ハンモック

　　いこくのかぜを

　　　　ゆらしたり

季語　　ハンモック（夏）

Hanmokku

    ikoku no kaze o

        urashi tari

The hammock

    is rocking in the wind

        from foreign countries

Season word: *hanmokku* (hammock; summer)

巴里祭や

　　猫も鼠も

　　　　バスティーユ

パリさいや

　　ねこもねずみも

　　　　バスティーユ

季語　巴里祭（パリ祭、フランス革命記念日、夏）

パリ祭は、1789年7月14日パリの民衆がバスティーユ監

獄に集まり、フランス革命の発端となった歴史を記念する

フランスの祝日。1790年のフランス建国記念祭が起源。

Pari sai ya

neko mo nezumi mo

Basutiiyu

At the Paris Festival

everyone, cats and mice,

goes to the Bastille

Season word: *Pari sai* (Paris Festival, or Bastille Day, July

14; summer)

The Paris Festival is the Japanese name for Bastille Day,

the French National Festival in commemoration of the

historic event of the Storming of the Bastille on July 14,

1789, which initiated the French Revolution.

サングラス

　　曇る心を

　　　　隠したり

サングラス

　　くもるこころを

　　　　かくしたり

季語　　サングラス（夏）

San gurasu

kumoru kokoro o

kakushi tari

The sunglasses

are hiding

the cloudy hearts of people

Season word: *san gurasu* (sunglasses; summer)

山開き

　　リュックの背負ふ

　　　記憶かな

やまびらき

　　リュックのせおう

　　　きおくかな

季語　　山開き（夏）

Yama biraki

ryukku no seou

kioku kana

At the opening of the mountaineering season

the backpack carries

memories of the past

Season word: *yama biraki* (opening of the mountaineering

season; summer)

阿智の夏

　　アマチュア

　　　天体観測し

あちのなつ

　　アマチュアてんたい

　　　かんそくし

　　　　　　　　.

季語　　夏（夏）

長野県阿智村は、近年、天体観測の人気スポットとなる。

Achi no natsu

    amachua tentai

        kansoku shi

In the summer at Achi

    amateurs are enjoying

        astronomical observations

Season word: *natsu* (summer; summer)

Achi village, Nagano prefecture, is located in the Japan
Alps, and has become a popular destination for amateur
astronomical observations.

August

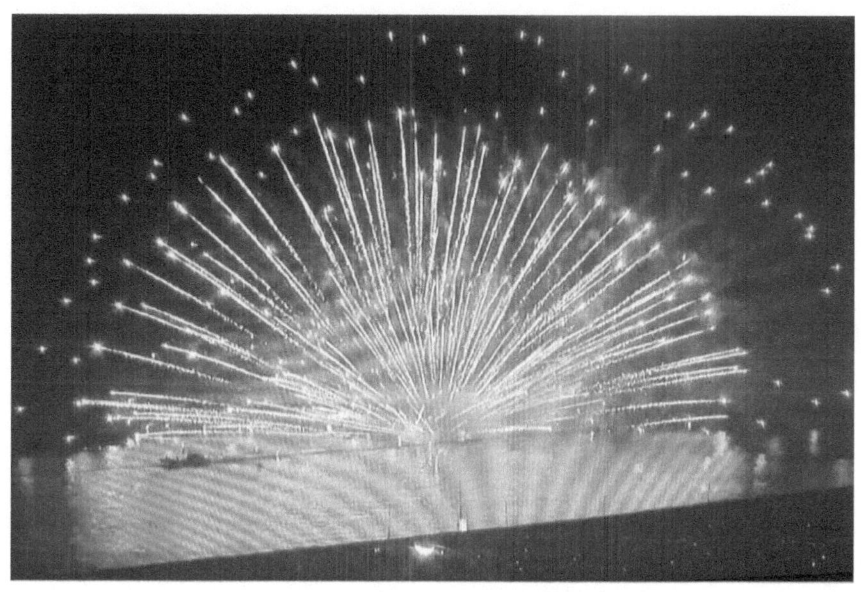

Photograph 8. Kumano Grand Fireworks Festival, Kumano,

Mie prefecture, taken by the author

大花火

　　熊野の神も

　　　　唸りたり

おおはなび

　　くまののかみも

　　　　うなりたり

季語　　大花火（夏）

三重県熊野市の七里御浜で毎年8月に開催される熊野大
花火大会を詠む。近くに、熊野三山がある。

Ō hanabi

Kumano no kami mo

unari tari

The Grand Fireworks Festival

even made the gods in Kumano

roar in awe

Season word: *hanabi* (fireworks; summer)

The Kumano Grand Fireworks Festival is conducted at

Shichiri mihama beach in Kumano, Mie prefecture,

annually in August. The locale is one of the most sacred

places in Japan, with three Kumano Grand Shrines nearby.

花火散り

　　水面の月の

　　　　戻りたり

はなびちり

　　みなものつきの

　　　　もどりたり

季語　花火（夏）

Hanabi chiri

minamo no tsuki no

modori tari

The fireworks have fallen

and the moon is shining

again on the water

Season word: *hanabi* (fireworks; summer)

吾子巣立つ

　　空つぽの空

　　　　夏の空

あこすだつ

　　からっぽのそら

　　　　なつのそら

季語　夏の空（夏）

Ako sudatsu

karappono sora

natsu no sora

My child has fledged

emptiness spreads

in the summer sky

Season word: *natsu no sora* (summer sky; summer)

夏休み

　　教室の時計

　　　独り待つ

なつやすみ

　　きょうしつのとけい

　　　ひとりまつ

季語　夏休み（夏）

Natsu yasumi

    kyōshitsu no tokei

        hitori matsu

The summer recess

    the clock in the classroom

        waits alone

Season word: *natsu yasumi* (summer recess; summer)

This situation is more prominent in the schools in

Fukushima where residents had been evacuated in the wake

of the meltdowns of the Fukushima Daiichi Nuclear Power

Station. More than seven years later, residents have not

returned and schools there are left abandoned.

夏祭り

　　綿菓子しぼみ

　　　　蝉しきり

なつまつり

　　わたがししぼみ

　　　　せみしきり

季語　夏祭り（夏）　蝉（夏）

Natsu matsuri

watagashi shibomi

semi shikari

The summer night festival

the cotton candy has shrunk

and the cicada cries incessantly

Season words: *natsu matsuri* (summer night festival;

summer) and *semi* (cicada; summer)

金魚すくふ

　　手を見る寺の

　　　　子猫かな

きんぎょすくう

　　ておみるてらの

　　　　こねこかな

季語　金魚すくい（夏）

寺の夜祭での光景。

Kingyo sukuu

te o miru tera no

koneko kana

The kitten at the temple

watches the hand

scooping up the goldfish

Season word: *kingyo sukui* (goldfish scooping; summer)

Scooping up goldfish with a thin paper scoop from a water

tank is a popular game for children at summer night

festivals, which are often held on the premises of temples.

御巣鷹山

　　葉月の空の

　　　　悪夢なり

おすたかやま

　　はづきのそらの

　　　　あくむなり

季語　葉月（葉月は陰暦では秋、秋）

1985年8月12日の日本航空123便の事故現場は、群馬県上野村の御巣鷹山でなく、高天原山の尾根であるが、通称「御巣鷹の尾根」といわれる。

Osutaka yama

　　hazuki no sora no

　　　　akumu nari

Osutaka Ridge

　　remembers

　　　　the nightmare of the August sky

Season word: *Hazuki* (August in the lunar calendar; autumn)

On August 12, 1985, Japan Airlines Flight 123 crashed into two

ridges of Mt. Takamagahara in Ueno, Gunma prefecture. The

site is generally known as Osutaka Ridge of Mt. Osutaka. The

accident killed 520 people—including crew members and

passengers—out of a total of 524. This was the worst airplane

accident in Japan to date.

白百合の

　　訪問絶へぬ

　　　御巣鷹山

しらゆりの

　　ほうもんたえぬ

　　　おすたかやま

季語　白百合（夏）

毎年、8月12日には、遺族や関係者が御巣鷹山の事故

現場跡を訪れ、慰霊碑の前で祈りを捧げる。

Shirayuri no

 hōmon taenu

  Osutaka yama

The white lilies

 keep visiting Osutaka Ridge

  one after another

Season word: *shira yuri* (white lily; summer)

This is a memorial tribute to the tragic accident of Japan fines Flight 123 in 1985. Every year, on August 12, the victims' families visit the site and offer prayers at the memorial stone.

苧殻焚き

　　現世の憶ひ

　　　送り出す

おがらたき

　　げんせのおもい

　　　おくりだす

季語　苧殻焚き（秋）

Ogara taki

    genes no omoi

        okuri dasu

Burning peeled hemp stalks

    sends the memories of this world

        off to heaven

Season word: *ogara taki* (ritual of burning peeled hemp stalks; autumn)

It is a Buddhist custom to burn peeled hemp stalks during the Bon season, which falls on the week of August 15, in order to receive and send off the souls of ancestors who are believed to return to this world during the week.

精霊流し

　　爆竹弾け

　　　　霊の逝く

しょうりょうながし

　　ばくちくはじけ

　　　　れいのゆく

季語　精霊流し（秋）

Shōryō nagashi

bakuchiku hajike

rei no yuku

The ritual of the sending off of the souls

the firecrackers explode

and the souls depart

Season word: *shōryō nagashi* (the ritual of the sending off

of souls; autumn)

September

Photograph 9. Chrysanthemum dolls, under Creative Commons license, "Chrysanthemum Doll and Flower Festival, Gifu, Gifu prefecture," November 4, 2007, https://commons.wikimedia.org/wiki/File:Chrysanthemum_Doll_and_Flower_Festival_08.JPG

蝉籠に

　　木槿一挿し

　　　　風の声

せみかごに

　　むくげひとさし

　　　　かぜのこえ

季語　　木槿（秋）

千利休の孫で茶道の継承者千宗旦（1578年−1658年）
は、白木槿を好み（宗旦木槿）、蝉籠花入（せみかごはない
れ、蝉の形をした籐製の籠）に活けて、風情を醸し出した。

Semi kago ni

mukuge hitosashi

kaze no koe

In the cicada vase

a mukuge hibiscus was arranged

and the wind whispers

Season words: *mukuge* (rose of Sharon, Korean rose,

hibiscus syriacus; autumn)

The grandson of Sen no Rikyū (the master of the tea ceremony)

and his successor, Sen no Sōtan (1578–1658), favored white

mukuge, so that a species of white *mukuge* is called *Sōtan

mukuge. Semi kago* (*lit.*, cicada basket"), a wicker vase in the

shape of a cicada, is used in the tea ceremony.

蜻蛉や

　　女人の哀れ

　　　　綴りたり

かげろうや

　　にょにんのあわれ

　　　　つづりたり

季語　蜻蛉（秋）

藤原道綱の母（936年頃−995年）の記した『蜻蛉日記』に寄せて。

Kagerō ya

    nyonin no aware

        tsuzuri tari

The mayfly

    is writing

        the sad life of the woman

Season word: *kagerō* (mayfly; autumn)

Mayflies are aquatic insects belonging to the order of

ephemeroptera and are known for brief lives. This haiku is

an allusion to *Kagerō nikki* (Diary of the Mayfly) written

by Fujiwara no Michitsuna's mother (her name is

unknown, circa 936–995). Her poems are compiled in

famous anthologies of the Heian period.

白露の日

　　物干し竿の

　　　　貰ひ泣き

はくろのひ

　　ものほしざおの

　　　　もらいなき

季語　　白露の日（秋）

白露の日は9月8日頃に始まり、期間としては9月22日頃

まで続く。白露の朝に洗濯物を干す主婦の心境。

Hakuro no hi

monohoshi zao no

morai naki

The Day of White Dew

the laundry drying rod

is crying with the mother

Season word: *Hakuro* (*lit.*, "white dew," the time of

morning dew; autumn)

In the 24-point solar terms, *Hakuro* refers to the fifteenth

point among the 24, which usually begins on September 8

and lasts until September 22. Japanese mothers hang

laundry on drying rods outdoors even on cold mornings.

祖母の亡き

　　敬老の日や

　　　　乳母車

そぼのなき

　　けいろうのひや

　　　　うばぐるま

季語　敬老の日（秋）

祖母が生前、外出時に体を支えるために使っていた乳母車の思い出。

Sobo no naki

Keirō no hi ya

uba guruma

The Day of the Elderly

without the grandmother

the stroller is left behind

Season word: *Keirō no hi* (Day of the Elderly; autumn)

A grandmother used to use a stroller to support her body when she walked.

菊の香や

　　門の扉を

　　　　開け放つ

きくのかや

　　もんのとびらを

　　　　あけはなつ

季語　菊（秋）

Kiku no ka ya

    mon no tobira o

        ake hanatsu

The scent of the chrysanthemum

    opens

        the gate

Season word: *kiku* (chrysanthemum; autumn)

菊人形

　　城の主人と

　　　　なりにけり

きくにんぎょう

　　しろのあるじと

　　　　なりにけり

季語　菊人形（秋）

Kiku ningyō

shiro no aruji to

narini keri

The chrysanthemum doll

has become

the lord of the castle

Season word: *kiku* (chrysanthemum; autumn)

The display of spectacular life-size dolls made of

chrysanthemums is a highlight of chrysanthemum festivals

in Japan.

菊膾

　　一夜に消えし

　　　　庭の色と香

きくなます

　　いちやにきえし

　　　　にわのいろとか

季語　菊膾（秋）

米国に住む日本人が自宅の庭に咲いた菊を食べてしまい、

隣の米婦人が、菊の花が突然消えてしまったことを訝しん

だという実話。

Kiku namasu

ichiya ni kieshi

niwa no iro to ka

The pickled chrysanthemum

the color and scent in the garden

disappeared overnight

Season word: *kiku* (chrysanthemum; autumn)

The Japanese pickle chrysanthemum flowers and eat them
as a seasonal delicacy. An American woman was puzzled
by the overnight disappearance of the chrysanthemums
from her Japanese neighbor's garden.

彼岸花

　　生き写しの児

　　　　歩きたり

ひがんばな

　　いきうつしのこ

　　　　あるきたり

季語　彼岸花(秋)

Higan bana

    iki utsushi no ko

        aruki tari

In the field of red spider lilies

    a child who looks like my dead child

        is walking

Season word: *higan bana* (red spider lily; autumn)

The red spider lily is called *higan bana* (*lit*, "the autumnal equinox flower") because it blooms in the season of the autumnal equinox when people visit their ancestral graves and pay tribute to the souls of the deceased in the family.

レモン・ティー

　　　一滴の香り

　　　　一滴の癒し

レモン・ティー

　　　いってきのかおり

　　　　いってきのいやし

季語　レモン（秋）

Remon tii

    itteki no kaori

        itteki no iyashi

Into the tea

    a drop of lemon goes

        and out comes a sip of solace

Season word: *remon* (lemon; autumn)

長き夜は

　　無伴奏チェロ

　　　奏でたり

ながきよは

　　むばんそうチェロ

　　　かなでたり

季語　長き夜〔秋〕

無伴奏チェロは、J. S. バッハの「無伴奏チェロ組曲」を指
す。第一番から第六番まで全6曲ある。

Nagaki yo wa

   mubansō chero

      kanade tari

The long autumn night

   one is playing

      the unaccompanied cello suite

Season word: *nagaki yo* (long autumn night; autumn)

The unaccompanied cello suite refers to the six Cello

Suites, BWV 1007–1012, of J. S. Bach.

October

Photograph 10. Scarecrow and pumpkins, taken by the author

異邦人

　　案山子の里の

　　　　迎へたり

いほうじん

　　かかしのさとの

　　　　むかえたり

季語　　案山子（秋）

四国徳島県三好市東祖谷の名頃地区は「限界集落」で、

2017年7月時点の人口は29人であった。住民の代わり

に、人間そっくりの、まるで生きているかのような案山子が

180体置かれる。「渓谷の人形」として海外に紹介される。

Ihōjin

    kakashi no sato no

        mukae tari

The foreign visitor

    is being welcomed

        by the scarecrows in the village

Season word: *kakashi* (scarecrows; autumn)

Nagoro village in Higashi-Iya, Miyoshi, Tokushima prefecture, has become famous as the "Village of Scarecrows." In July 2017, more than 180 scarecrow dolls that look like live human beings were placed in the village of population 29. A German photojournalist introduced this village as "Valley of Dolls: Japan's Disappearing Villages," attracting foreign tourists.

廃校や

　　案山子の生徒

　　　授業受け

はいこうや

　　かかしのせいと

　　　じゅぎょううけ

季語　案山子（秋）

四国徳島県三好市東祖谷の名頃地区の「案山子の里」に
は、現在子供は一人もいない。廃校となった教室には、案
山子の生徒が座っている。

Haikō ya

kakashi no seito

jugyō uke

In the empty abandoned school

scarecrows

are attending the class

Season word: *kakashi* (scarecrows; autumn)

No child lives in Nagoro village now. In place of children, *kakashi* dolls are sitting in a classroom of an abandoned school.

鰯雲

　　築地最後の

　　　　一本締め

いわしぐも

　　つきじさいごの

　　　　いっぽんじめ

季語　鰯雲（秋）

2018年10月6日、世界最大の魚市場、築地市場が83年の幕
を閉じた。関係者は涙を禁じ得なかった。東京都知事選を巻き
込む大論争の末、豊洲に移転が決まったが、その後も問題が
続出し、2016年11月の移転予定が大幅に遅れた。

Iwashi gumo

    Tsukiji saigo no

        ippon jime

The sardine clouds

    the last clapping

        at the Tsukiji Fish Market

Season word: *iwashi gumo* (sardine-like clouds; autumn)

On October 6, 2018, the Tsukiji Fish Market ended its 83

years of operation, to be transferred to nearby Toyosu, after

much controversy involving the Tokyo governor elections.

"Ippon jime" is the ceremonial, rhythmic hand clapping

performed at the conclusion of a special event.

秋暁や

　　ターレのうねり

　　　　海何想ふ

しゅうぎょうや

　　ターレのうねり

　　　　うみなにおもう

季語　　秋暁（秋）

2018年10月、築地市場から新豊洲市場に移転の際、夜明け前に何十ものターレ（荷役用の小型運搬車、魚運搬に使われる）が列をなして築地大橋、黎明大橋、豊洲大橋を渡り、築地から豊洲に移動する様は感動的であった。

Shūgyō ya

    tāre no uneri

        umi nani omou

The autumn dawn

    what is the sea thinking

        watching the waves of electric carts

Season word: *shūgyō* (autumn dawn; autumn)

With the Tsukiji Fish Market closed, countless electric

carts carrying seafood moved to the new Toyosu Fish

Market at dawn, crossing the Sumida River via the Tsukiji

Grand Bridge, the Reimei Grand Bridge, and the Toyosu

Grand Bridge. It was a spectacular and moving sight.

濁り酒

　　　音信川の

　　　　　匂ひ立つ

にごりざけ

　　　おとずれがわの

　　　　　においたつ

季語　濁り酒（秋）

山口県長門市の湯本温泉は、音信川（おとずれがわ）の
遊歩道沿いに設けられた「おとずれ足湯」で有名。

Nigori zake

    Otozure gawa no

        nioi tatsu

The unfiltered sake

    fills the air

        over the Otozure River

Season word: *nigori zake* (unfiltered sake; autumn)

The Nagato–Yumoto hot spring resort in Nagato,

Yamaguchi prefecture, is famous for outdoor footbaths

installed along the Otozure River.

宿の女将

　　ソムリエのごと

　　　　新酒注ぐ

やどのおかみ

　　ソムリエのごと

　　　　しんしゅつぐ

季語　新酒（秋）

Yado no okami

somurie no goto

shinshu tsugu

The inn's proprietress

is pouring the newly brewed sake

as if she were a sommelier

Season word: *shinshu* (newly brewed sake; autumn)

「赤い羽根」

　　母の羽織に

　　　　潜みたり

あかいはね

　　ははのはおりに

　　　　ひそみたり

季語　「赤い羽根」（赤い羽根共同募金運動、秋）

赤い羽根共同募金運動は、毎年10月1日から月末まで行
われる。

Akai hane

    haha no haori ni

        hisomi tari

The "red feather"

    was hiding

        in the kimono jacket of the dead mother

Season word: *akai hane* (*lit.*, "red feather" refers to the Red Feather Fundraising; autumn)

The "red feather" is the symbol of the annual fundraising campaign in October of the Central Community Chest of Japan, which is part of the United Way Worldwide.

栃の実を

　　数へて遊ぶ

　　　　母亡き子

とちのみを

　　かぞえてあそぶ

　　　　ははなきこ

季語　栃の実（秋）

妻を二度亡くした物理学者で作家の寺田寅彦（1878年
－1935年）のエッセイ集『橡の実』に寄せて。

Tochi no mi o

kazoete asobu

haha naki ko

The motherless child

is playing

counting the horse chestnuts

Season word: *tochi no mi* (horse chestnuts; autumn)

This is a homage to the essay anthology, *Tochi no mi*

(Horse Chestnuts), written by the physicist/writer Terada

Torahiko (1878–1935), who lost his wife twice.

栃餅や

　　実を割る素手の

　　　　皺深し

とちもちや

　　みをわるすでの

　　　　しわふかし

季語　栃餅（秋）

母を亡くした子のために、栃餅を作る祖母の姿。固い栃の
実を割るのは大変な作業である。

Tochi mochi ya

    mi o waru sude no

        shiwa fukashi

Tochi mochi cooking

    the hand cracking the horse chestnuts

        has deep wrinkles

Season word: *tochi mochi* (steamed rice cake with horse chestnuts; autumn)

A grandmother is making steamed rice cakes with horse chestnuts for a motherless child. It is a hard work to crack chestnuts.

ハロウィーン

　　南瓜畑の

　　　　淋しかり

ハロウィーン

　　かぼちゃばたけの

　　　　さみしかり

季語　ハロウィーン（秋）　南瓜（秋）

Harowiin

kabocha batake no

samishi kari

Halloween

the pumpkin field

must be feeling lonely

Season words: *Harowiin* (Halloween; autumn) and

kabocha (pumpkin; autumn)

November

Photograph 11. Traditional Japanese sandals made of rice

straw, taken by the author

黒葡萄

　　ボジョレ・ヌーボーに

　　早変わり

くろぶどう

　　ボジョレ・ヌーボーに

　　はやがわり

季語　黒葡萄（秋）

ボジョレ・ヌーボーは、毎年11月第三木曜日が解禁日とな

る。2018年の解禁日は、11月15日。

Kuro budō

    Bojore nūbō ni

        haya gawari

The black grape

    has quickly transformed itself

        into Beaujolais Nouveau

Season word: *kuro budō* (black grapes; autumn)

Beaujolais Nouveau is released on the third Thursday of November. The first shipment of Beaujolais Nouveau brings the excitement of the season to Japan. The release date for 2018 is November 15.

「一葉忌」

　　赤き鼻緒の

　　　　切れし橋

いちようき

　　あかきはなおの

　　　　きれしはし

季語　「一葉忌」（11月23日、冬）

11月23日は、樋口一葉（1872年−1896年）の命日。

Ichiyō ki

akaki hanao no

kireshi hashi

On the memorial day of Ichiyō

the bridge is reminiscing about

the broken red strap of the wooden clog

Season word: *Ichiyō-ki* (anniversary memorial day of

Higuchi Ichiyō's death, November 23; winter)

Higuchi Ichiyō (1872–1896) was a female writer, who died

young of tuberculosis.

初霜や

　　太極拳の

　　　　息白し

はつしもや

　　たいきょくけんの

　　　　いきしろし

季語　初霜（冬）　息白し（冬）

太極拳の早朝稽古。

Hatsu shimo ya

    Taikyoku ken no

        iki shiro shi

In the first frost

    the Taichi practitioner

        is exhaling white air

Season word: *hatsu shimo* (first frost of the season; winter)

The scene describes the Taichi practice in the early morning.

日向ぼこ

　　お日様と話す

　　　　車椅子

ひなたぼこ

　　おひさまとはなす

　　　　くるまいす

季語　日向ぼこ（冬）

Hinata boko

ohisama to hanasu

kuruma isu

Basking in the winter sun

the wheelchair

is talking with the sun

Season word: *hinata boto* (winter sun-bathing; winter)

This scene describes a patient in his wheelchair basking in
the sun in winter.

小春日や

　　父に手紙を

　　　　読み聞かせ

こはるびや

　　ちちにてがみを

　　　　よみきかせ

季語　小春日（冬）

妹が父に米国からの手紙を読んでやっている様子。

Koharu bi ya

    chichi ni tegami o

        yomi kikase

On an Indian Summer day

    the daughter is reading

        a letter to her father

Season word: *koharu bi* (*lit.*, "little spring day," a fine warm day in early winter, Indian Summer; winter) The term *koharu* (*lit.*, "little spring") refers to October in the lunar calendar, which signifies an early winter. This haiku describes a scene in which my sister is reading a letter from the United States to my father.

湯冷めした

　　父にココアを

　　　　すすめたり

ゆざめした

　　ちちにココアを

　　　　すすめたり

季語　湯冷め（冬）　ココア（冬）

Yuzame shita

chichi ni kokoa o

susume tari

The daughter is making

hot cocoa for her father

who felt an afterbath chill

Season words: *yuzame* (afterbath chill; winter) and *kokoa*

(hot cocoa; winter)

あかぎれを

　　叱られ泣く子

　　　　水の冷たし

あかぎれを

　　しかられなくこ

　　　　みずのつめたし

季語　　あかぎれ（冬）　冷たし（冬）

どれだけよく手を拭いてもあかぎれができて、いつも母に
叱られた想い出。

Akagire o

    shikarare naku ko

        mizu no tsumetashi

The girl who was scolded

    for the chapping on her hands

        feels the water even colder

Season words: *akagire* (chapping; winter) and *tsumetashi* (cold; winter)

My mother used to scold me for the bad chapping on my hands. She thought that I had not dried my hands well, contrary to the facts. I had sensitive hands and no matter how well I dried my hands, I had chapping and bleeding on them. No hot water taps existed at home in Japan when I was a child.

冬服の

　　ボタンを拾ふ

　　　　銀杏の葉

ふゆふくの

　　ボタンをひろう

　　　　いちょうのは

季語　冬服（冬）

銀杏（いちょう）の木は、季語ではない。銀杏の実（ギンナン）は、秋の季語である。

Fuyu fuku no

   botan o hirou

      ichō no ha

The ginko leaf

   is picking up the button

      that had dropped off from the winter clothes

Season word: *fuyu fuku* (winter clothes; winter)

A ginko (pronounced as "ichō") as a tree is not a season word, whereas a gingo nut (the same characters as the ginko tree but pronounced as "gin'nan") is a season word of autumn.

雪催ひ

　家路に急ぐ

　　ブーツかな

ゆきもよい

　いえじにいそぐ

　　ブーツかな

季語　雪催ひ（冬）

Yuki moyoi

   ieji ni isogu

      būtsu kana

Snow is coming

   and the boots are

      hurrying home

Season word: *būtsu* (boots; winter)

月明かり

　　かんじきの雪

　　　　トレッキング

つきあかり

　　かんじきのゆき

　　　　トレッキング

季語　かんじき（冬）　雪（冬）

近年、長野県八ヶ岳などで月明かりだけを頼りにするエコ・ツーリズム式の夜間トレッキングが人気となる。

Tsuki akari

    kanjiki no yuki

        trekkingu

Under the moonlight

    kanjiki snowshoes

        are trekking in the snow

Season words: *kanjiki* (traditional Japanese snowshoes; winter) and *yuki* (snow; winter)

In recent years, overnight trekking on the mountain snow under the moonlight without using any other light—a form of ecotourism—has become popular. The trekkers enjoy star gazing and wild animal encounters.

December

Photograph 12. Kadomatsu decoration for the new year,
under Creative Commons license, "Pair gate with [bamboo
and] pine branches for the new year, kadomatsu, Katori-
city, Japan," January 2, 2007
https://commons.wikimedia.org/wiki/File:Pair_gate_with_p
ine_branches_for_the_New_Year,kadomatsu,katori-
city,japan.JPG

笠地蔵

　　慈悲の心の

　　　　雪溶かし

かさじぞう

　　じひのこころの

　　　　ゆきとかし

季語　　雪（冬）

Kasa jizō

    jihi no kokoro no

        yuki tokasu

The old man had put his straw hats

    on the stone jizō statues

        and his benevolence melted the snow

Season word: *yuki* (snow; winter)

Kasa jizō (*lit.*, "straw-hat jizō") refers to a Japanese folk tale, in which

an old man felt sorry for the stone statues of the seven jizō (the

guardian gods of unborn children and their mothers), which were

exposed to snow on new year's eve, and put the straw hats he had made

for sale on the statues. He had only five straw hats, and he put his own

straw hat on the sixth jizō and his handkerchief on the seventh jizō, and

went home. He and his wife had no rice to celebrate the new year. At

night, the jizō statues brought fortune to his house in gratitude.

寒稽古

　　気合ひの音や

　　　　氷柱落つ

かんげいこ

　　きあいのおとや

　　　　つららおつ

季語　寒稽古（冬）　氷柱（冬）

Kan geiko

    kiai no oto ya

        tsurara otsu

During the winter training

    the sound of a spirited shout

        makes the icicles fall

Season words: *kan geiko* (winter training; winter) and *tsurara* (icicles; winter)

Kan geiko refers to training for mental and physical strength in winter, often performed in or near the freezing waterfalls.

紙ツリー

　　折るリハビリの

　　　　手の震へ

かみツリー

　　おるリハビリの

　　　　てのふるえ

季語　　紙ツリー（冬）

Kami tsurii

    oru rihabiri no

        te no furue

Making a paper Christmas tree

    the hands of the grandfather under rehabilitation

        are trembling

Season word: *kami tsurii* (paper Christmas tree; winter)

「漱石忌」

　　猫と一緒に

　　　　読書かな

そうせきき

　　ねこといっしょに

　　　　どくしょかな

季語　「漱石忌」（12月9日、冬）

夏目漱石（1867年−1916年）の命日は12月9日。漱石
の『吾輩は猫である』に寄せて。

Sōseki ki

   neko to issho ni

     dokusho kana

On the memorial day of Sōseki

   one is reading a book

     with a cat

Season word: *Sōseki-ki* (anniversary memorial day of

Natsume Sōseki's death, December 9; winter)

Natsume Soseki (1867–1916) wrote the popular novel,

Wagahai wa neko de aru (I Am a Cat).

漱石忌

　　『続　明暗』を

　　　　書き終へる

そうせきき

　　ぞくめいあんを

　　　　かきおえる

季語　漱石忌（12月9日、冬）

絶筆・未完となった漱石の『明暗』の続きを水村美苗が書
き、1990年に出版された。

Sōseki ki

    Zoku Meian o

        kaki oeru

On the memorial day of Sōseki

    one has finished writing

        Light and Darkness Continued

Season word: *Sōseki-ki* (anniversary memorial day of

Natsume Sōseki's death, December 9; winter)

Natsume Soseki died without finishing the novel *Meian*

(Light and Darkness). In 1990, the female writer

Mizumura Minae completed the novel.

歳末の

　　喧騒の聴く

　　　　静けさや

さいまつの

　　けんそうのきく

　　　　しずけさや

季語　歳末（冬）

歳末の雑踏の中に感じる静寂と孤独感。

Saimatsu no

kensō no kiku

shizukesa ya

The hustle and bustle of the year-end season

is listening

to the silence and solitude

Season word: *saimatsu* (year-end season; winter)

数へ日を

　　数へて淋し

　　　　異邦人

かぞえびを

　　かぞえてさびし

　　　　いほうじん

季語　数へ日（冬）

Kazoe bi o

    kazoe te sabishi

        ihōjin

Counting the remaining days of the year

    a foreigner

        feels lonely

Season word: *kazoe bi* (the remaining days of the year; winter)

Counting the remaining days of the year reminds a foreigner of his homeland, as the approaching new year is the most important yearly holiday in Japan, and families get together, as with Thanksgiving Day in the United States.

故郷の

　　匂ひほのかに

　　　　餅届き

ふるさとの

　　においほのかに

　　　　もちとどき

季語　　餅（冬）

Furusato no

   nioi honoka ni

      mocha todoki

The rice cakes

   have arrived

      with a faint scent of the hometown

Season word: *mochi* (rice cake; winter)

A family back home sends rice cakes to an expatriate for

the new year. Rice cakes are a must for the new year's

celebration in Japan.

師走の夜

　　「歓喜の歌」を

　　　　月詠ふ

しわすのよ

　　かんきのうたを

　　　　つきうたう

季語　師走の夜（冬）

年末に、ベートーベンの交響楽第九番を演奏することが

恒例となり、巷で「歓喜の歌」を練習する声が聴こえる。

Shiwasu no yo

Kanki no uta o

tsuki utau

On the night in December

the moon is reciting

the Ode to Joy

Season word: *shiwasu no yo* (a night in December; winter)

Since the 1980s it has become Japanese custom for amateur

singers to perform the choral Ode to Joy of the Ninth

Symphony of Ludwig van Beethoven at year-end concerts,

and they practice diligently in December.

門松立つ

　　明日の門出を

　　　　待ちにけり

かどまつたつ

　　あすのかどでを

　　　　まちにけり

季語　門松立つ（年末）

kadomatsu tatsu

asu no kadode o

machini keri

The kadomatsu is erected

and is waiting

for its debut tomorrow

Season word: *kado-matsu tatsu* (to erect pine ornaments at
the gate for the new year; year-end)

Kadomatsu is a traditional decoration for the new year,
made of pine, bamboo, and other plants, placed in pairs in
front of the gate or the entrance of the house.

About the author

Mayumi Itoh is a former Professor of Political Science at the University of Nevada, Las Vegas (UNLV). She has also taught at Princeton University and Queens College, City University of New York (CUNY), and has written numerous books and academic journal articles. Her book titles include:

–*Globalization of Japan: Japanese Sakoku Mentality and U.S. Efforts to Open Japan* (1998)

–*The Hatoyama Dynasty: Japanese Political Leadership Through the Generations* (2003)

–*Japanese War Orphans in Manchuria: Forgotten Victims of World War II* (2010)

–*Japanese Wartime Zoo Policy: The Silent Victims of World War II* (2010)

–*The Origin of Ping-Pong Diplomacy: The Forgotten Architect of Sino-U.S. Rapprochement* (2011)

–Pioneers of Sino-Japanese Relations: Liao and Takasaki

(2012)

–Hachi: The Truth of the Life and Legend of the Most

Famous Dog in Japan (2013)

–The Origins of Contemporary Sino-Japanese Relations:

Zhou Enlai and Japan (2016)

–The Making of China's War with Japan: Zhou Enlai and

Zhang Xueliang (2016)

–The Making of China's Peace with Japan: What Xi

Jinping Should Learn from Zhou Enlai (2017)

–"Hachi-ko" in Siberia: The True Story of Japanese

Prisoners of War and a Dog (2017)

–Hachiko: Solving Twenty Mysteries about the Most

Famous Dog in Japan (2017)

–Eliza Ruhamah Scidmore and Japan: The Life and Journeys to the Far East of the American Woman Who Brought "Sakura" to Washington, D.C. (2017)

–Kaneko Misuzu: Life and Poems of A Lonely Princes (2018)

–The Japanese Culture of Mourning Whales: Whale Graves and Memorial Monuments in Japan (2018)

–Haikus of All Seasons I: The Heavens and the Earth (2018)

–Animals and the Fukushima Nuclear Disaster (2018)

–Haikus of All Seasons II: Humanity (2018)

–Haikus of All Seasons III: Fauna (2018)

–Haikus of All Seasons IV: Flora (2018)

–Haikus of All Seasons V: The Heavens and the Earth (2018)

www.ingramcontent.com/pod-product-compliance
Lightning Source LLC
Chambersburg PA
CBHW031053250726

48655CB00004B/1421